CHARLES & DIANA

The 10th. Anniversary

BRIAN HOEY

Photography
Colour Library Books
The Glenn Harvey Picture Collection

Commissioning Editor
Andrew Preston

Commissioning
Edward Doling
Laura Potts

Editorial
Jane Adams

Production
Ruth Arthur
David Proffit
Sally Connolly
Andrew Whitelaw

Director of Production
Gerald Hughes

VIKING STUDIO BOOKS
Published by the Penguin Group
Viking Penguin, a division of
Penguin Books USA Inc., 375 Hudson Street,
New York, New York 10014, U.S.A.
Penguin Books Ltd, 27 Wrights Lane,
London W8 5TZ, England
Penguin Books Australia Ltd, Ringwood,
Victoria, Australia
Penguin Books Canada Ltd, 2801 John Street,
Markham, Ontario, Canada L3R 1B4
Penguin Books (N.Z.) Ltd, 182-190 Wairau Road,
Auckland 10, New Zealand

Penguin Books Ltd, Registered Offices:
Harmondsworth, Middlesex, England

First Published in 1991 in the United States
of America by Viking Penguin, a division of
Penguin Books USA Inc. and in Great Britain
by Colour Library Books.

10 9 8 7 6 5 4 3 2 1

CLB 2671
© 1991 Colour Library Books Ltd, Godalming,
Surrey, England
All rights reserved

CIP data available
ISBN 0-670-83948-5
Printed in Italy
Set in Cheltenham

CHARLES & DIANA
The 10th. Anniversary

BRIAN HOEY

VIKING STUDIO BOOKS

Ten Glorious Years

Since their wedding on 29 July, 1981, the Prince and Princess of Wales have matured from fairy-tale bride and groom into two of the most popular and hard-working members of the Royal Family. Built up over the ten years of their marriage, this strong partnership is the perfect base for moving forward together to face the decades that lie ahead.

Left: Highgrove House, the Prince and Princess of Wales' country home in Gloucestershire to which they retreat as often as possible.

In the ten years that they have been married, the Prince and Princess of Wales have become the focus of public attention to an extent never before experienced in Britain, even by the Royal Family.

As they begin their second decade together, they remain the most closely watched couple in the world and the interest they inspire in the media, and in ordinary people throughout the world, continues unabated. For this is a phenomenon that is not confined to Britain alone. In May 1990, the Prince and Princess made their first official visit to Eastern Europe. The wife of the President of Hungary was so overcome at being in the royal presence that she broke down and began to cry. She was comforted by a caring – and much younger – Princess of Wales, who simply took her hand and smiled. It was a tiny but significant example of the way in which the woman who will be the next Queen Consort of England has matured into the self-confident and relaxed person that she is today.

Her Royal Highness has coped in an exemplary fashion with the rigid structure of life at court and has shown good-humoured, if at times resigned, tolerance towards the obsessive attentions of the ever-intrusive media.

When Prince Charles was single, he was considered to be the most eligible bachelor in the world and, as heir to the throne, he was used to being in the spotlight. However, nothing he had experienced in previous years compared with the mass adulation and widespread fascination he and his wife attracted at and after their wedding in St Paul's Cathedral on 29 July, 1981.

Together they were feted wherever they went,

The three-year-old Lady Diana Spencer sits in her pram at Park House, Sandringham, in Norfolk.

Once the news broke that Lady Diana Spencer was Prince Charles' new romance, press cameramen pursued her relentlessly. They beseiged her at her London flat at Coleherne Court and at her work at the Young England kindergarten in Pimlico and followed her everywhere. It was a difficult time for Lady Diana, but she coped remarkably well. Prince Charles had been coping with press attention all his life.

becoming the most sought-after couple on earth, and within a short period the Princess of Wales became the most photographed woman in the world, eclipsing every other member of the Royal Family in the amount of public interest she generated – in her dress, her tastes, what she said and even what she ate.

Throughout the world, presidents and prime ministers vied with each other in their efforts to persuade the royal couple to visit them. Politicians of every hue wanted to be photographed in their presence, knowing that any picture of Diana was going to be featured prominently in national newspapers and glossy

An official portrait of Lady Diana by Bryan Organ was later slashed, but repaired.

magazines. If Prince Charles arrived at a function without his wife at his side, his hosts tried hard not to show their disappointment too much. Prince Charles himself quickly realised that it was the Princess everybody wanted to see and he, with wry good humour, took a back seat, saying: 'I know it's my wife you want – not me.' In the comparatively short time that she has been Princess of Wales, Diana has endowed the position with extraordinary dignity and grace – and also with a glamour few would have forecast when she first came to the public notice barely ten years ago. She has taken what is at best an ill-defined job and given it a modern twist. At the same time she has managed, with considerable skill, to combine

From 'Shy Di' to glowing fiancée, the change is obvious. As Prince Charles' fiancée, Lady Diana attended her first public engagements and there were hints of the glamorous sensation she was to become.

**The happy couple pose for photographs on the garden steps at
Buckingham Palace after the announcment of their engagement.**

Lady Diana's magnificent ivory silk taffeta gown, a well kept secret, and the bridesmaids' dresses were designed by David and Elizabeth Emanuel. Below: the marriage register.

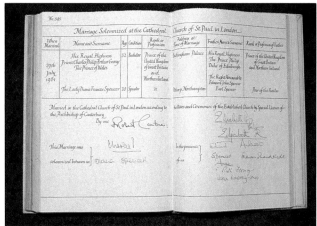

the roles of wife, mother and the most public of figures, while rarely putting a foot wrong as a representative of the younger generation of royals.

In fact it has been claimed that her natural charm and unfeigned beauty have added a new dimension to the monarchy. She has certainly been responsible for a massive increase in interest in the Royal Family. In short, she has 'star quality'.

The Prince and Princess of Wales are a superb team; they complement each other perfectly in spite of a twelve-year age difference. Perhaps one of the most important qualities they share is a sense of humour. Prince Charles once said: 'The most important thing a person in my position can have is a sense of humour … being able to laugh at oneself.' The Princess has said since her marriage: 'If we couldn't see the funny side of things sometimes, we'd go crazy.'

**Lady Diana wore the Spencer family diamond tiara to hold her veil in place
and made a breathtaking, fairy-tale bride.**

If there is one aspect of their marriage which has perhaps not worked out entirely to their joint satisfaction it is that the generation gap between them has not narrowed. Just before they were married Prince Charles said: 'She will keep me young.' She hasn't. He is regarded as someone who is rather old for his years – some unkind critics have said that he was 'born middle-aged' – and, in spite of the efforts of his wife to update his image, he has

Vast crowds lined the route of the wedding procession and pressed against the railings at Buckingham Palace to cheer the royal newlyweds. The Prince and Princess of Wales returned from St Paul's Cathedral in a 1902 landau.

remained what he has always been: a conservative, serious-minded man who regards duty as a sacred trust to be preserved above all other emotions – including love!

The Princess of Wales has become a most self-assured twenty-nine-year-old, and even the birth of her two children and an increasing royal workload have not diminished her zest for life. She is as energetic as ever and the realization that she has become one of the most sought-after women in the world has given her tremendous confidence and the ability to be thoroughly modern, without for a moment losing any of the magic that members of the Royal Family must retain at all times.

After ten years of marriage, the Prince and Princess have settled into what has been described as 'an affectionate accommodation'. They are very fond of each other and are both totally devoted to their children. Prince Charles is still as inflexible as he has always been, but he has now found his role in life, and this has given him an inner peace and tranquility. The Princess has been transformed from the starry-eyed young girl who was bowled over when she was proposed to by the future king to a pragmatic yet happy woman who is content with her small family and secure in the knowledge that her destiny is to sit alongside her husband on the throne. Princess Diana has proved that she is a survivor,

Above left: the newlyweds leave Buckingham Palace in a balloon-decorated carriage for their honeymoon. This began at Broadlands, the Hampshire home of the late Lord Mountbatten, where the Queen and Prince Philip also spent part of their honeymoon. Remaining pictures: they then flew to Gibraltar to join Her Majesty's Royal Yacht *Britannia* for a cruise in the Mediterranean.

and together the Prince and Princess have managed to weather the storms of public criticism that plagued the early years of their marriage. Theirs is now a partnership of understanding, companionship and true affection.

The workload of the Prince and Princess is staggering. It would be impossible for them to accept even a quarter of the 50,000 requests and invitations that flood into their office at St James's Palace every year. More people and organizations want to see them than they do any other member of the Royal Family and between them they receive more invitations than the others put together.

The life style of the Prince and Princess of Wales is extraordinary even by royal standards. As one of the richest men in the world, Prince Charles can afford anything he or his family wants, and they do not stint themselves. Their homes, in Kensington Palace and,

Glowing with happiness, Charles and Diana returned from their cruise to spend the last part of their honeymoon at Balmoral, where they posed for photographers.

Glamorous nights for the royal couple; dancing is the Princess's great passion. She loves ballet, jazz and tap and wanted to be a professional dancer, but she grew too tall.

even more so, at Highgrove House contain every conceivable luxury, and everything that they eat, drink, wear or otherwise use is the very best that money can buy.

Prince Charles is an old-style aristocrat who grew up surrounded by servants. There were always butlers and footmen at his beck and call, a valet to supervise his wardrobe and chauffeurs to drive him wherever he wanted to go. When he wanted to learn to drive, fly, make a parachute descent or paint, or to study music, architecture or literature, the finest tutors in the land were on hand to make sure his instruction was of the very best.

The Princess grew up in a different manner. She too came from a privileged background, with nannies and nurses, maids and governesses. But she was never aware of being able to ask for anything she wanted and it being immediately available. And of course, as a child she was never the focus of public attention that her husband was.

When she moved away from the family home to live in a flat in London with three friends, it gave her a glimpse of the outside world her husband has never known. She is surely the only future Queen of England who has ever worked as a 'charlady', mopping floors and washing dishes. During her bachelor-girl days, she also pushed a trolley around the local supermarket where she did her weekly shopping and used public transport to get around London.

All this helped to shape the personality that has since emerged. In the ten years that she has been Princess of Wales she has adapted to the ways of the Royal Family brilliantly, yet without losing any of her own independence of spirit. She is, in every way, her own woman. It has not been an entirely easy path and, in the

The Princess enjoys some fun at the races with the Duchess of York. In June, Diana regularly attends the annual Royal Ascot race meeting, which is famous as a fashion mecca, especially on Ladies' Day.

early days, Her Royal Highness went through a number of difficult periods as she tried to come to grips with being both a working member of the Royal Family and a young wife.

Her husband may have been used to the unrelenting glare of the spotlight, but it was something she had to learn to cope with and it did not come easily or quickly. There were also problems concerning the purely domestic side of their life together. Prince Charles had grown up in a well-ordered environment where things

The royal couple leave hospital proudly with their second son, Prince Harry, shortly after he was born in September 1984.

Prince William was the first heir presumptive to be delivered in hospital.

Prince Charles quickly became a doting father, while the Princess is a natural mother, who regards her children's welfare as her top priority and broke with tradition by taking baby William on an overseas tour.

rarely changed. He did not take a great deal of interest in how his household worked as long as it did work, and perfectly. After his marriage he wanted this state of affairs to continue and saw no reason why it should not. However, his new wife was a woman with her own ideas – about style, food and furniture and especially about who was going to be working for them. In his bachelor days, the Prince employed a small clique of servants who had been with him for many years and who knew exactly how he liked his life arranged. When the Princess came along she resented the 'old guard' – and they resented her – and she quickly set about replacing them with appointments of her own. This resulted in a rapid

turnover of staff in the early months, although this was not nearly as rapid as press reports at the time made out.

The Princess set out to transform the apartment in Kensington Palace and the house in Gloucestershire into homes that would be both the epitome of gracious living, as demanded by Prince Charles, and a reflection of her own personality and generation. She refused to compromise – on decoration, furniture, materials or cost

Unlike most of the Royal Family, Diana does not like riding. However, she has supported Prince Charles in his passion for polo by watching him play since before their marriage.

– and the result is the creation of two of the most outstanding examples of what a modern young woman can achieve when she is allowed to combine her own ideas with the expertise of some of the design world's most innovative and exciting talents.

On her own admission the Princess of Wales is not an intellectual; her scholastic record is evidence of her lack of academic achievement. However, she does possess a native wit and intelligence which have served her to good purpose in the years since she became public property in 1981. If she had been, as she was occasionally described, merely a 'walking clotheshorse', she would never have survived those early days nor adapted to her role in the way she has. The way in which she has taught herself to cope with the burdens of public office when it seemed, for a time at least, that she might succumb, is proof of her determination to succeed in all she attempts. Her charm is apparent to all; what is not quite so obvious is the iron will that has turned her from a shy, blushing

teenager into a confident, beautiful woman who is also a fully paid-up member of the 'Royal Firm', as King George VI once described the working members of the Royal Family.

The main reason why the Prince and Princess of Wales have been so successful as a partnership is that they have managed to achieve that most difficult of combinations – a high-profile public life and a secure family background.

The Princess, although she shares an extraordinary sense of duty with her husband, has made no secret of the fact that she considers the most important events of her life so far to be the births of her two children. She is a natural mother who believes that the welfare of her children is her number one priority – something which became obvious shortly after the birth of Prince William. The Prince and Princess were going to Australia on an extended visit, and Her Royal Highness insisted on taking their infant son with them. She was not going to be separated from her baby for such a long period and thereby miss what she regarded as a most important part of his early life. This was a departure from normal royal behaviour – both Prince Charles and Princess Anne had been left behind by their parents for months at a time

The royal couple often tour abroad and Diana always has to dress appropriately. On their six-day visit to Kuwait and the United Arab Emirates in 1989, that meant covering up. The Princess appears to have less difficulty sitting cross-legged than her husband.

The Princess wore this blue and white trouser outfit to sit on suchions for a lunch – a magnificent Bedouin feast at a desert oasis near Al Ain.

during the first years of their lives – and it earned for the Princess the approval of many young mothers who sympathized with her dilemma. As for the Princess herself, it showed that she did have a mind of her own and was not prepared to be merely a pretty accessory.

Although Lady Diana Spencer first met the man who was to become her husband when she was just a young girl living in a grace-and-favour house in the grounds of Sandringham House, the first hint of romance between the couple was not until July 1980 – exactly a year before they were married.

During Cowes Week, Diana was invited as a guest on board the Royal Yacht *Britannia*, by Prince Philip. There was nothing unusual in this. Both the Queen and Prince Philip often included young ladies on their guest lists, so nobody thought anything of it. The following month

though, she turned up again at a royal party; this time it was a much more important occasion – the eightieth birthday celebrations for Queen Elizabeth the Queen Mother. This invitation was issued at the request of Prince Charles himself – it was the first time he had ever asked for a young woman to be included in what was essentially a family affair.

Within weeks their relationship had blossomed as Lady Diana joined the rest of the Royal Family at Balmoral where she and Charles spent many happy hours together discovering their mutual interests and their love for each other.

Almost from the day she became a member of the Royal Family, the elegant Princess became a leader of British fashion, and she has since set new standards in royal style. She has given an enormous boost to the fashion industry at home, and been acclaimed as the world's best-dressed woman.

Prince William was a very lively toddler. Diana, who had suffered badly from morning sickness, said after his birth: 'It's amazing how much happiness a small child brings to people.' William showed an early interest in kicking a ball around and later became a keen footballer at Wetherby pre-prep school in Notting Hill. During their children's early years, the Prince and Princess of Wales made sure that they could see as much as possible of their sons by sending them to schools close to Kensington Palace.

Diana's father, the eighth Earl Spencer, had spent much of his life in royal service, as equerry first to King George VI and then to the latter's daughter, when she became Queen Elizabeth II.

He lived, with his then wife and their children, in Park House, one of many spacious homes on the royal estate at Sandringham. The house had been built by Edward VII as a guest house for his many friends, who could not all be accommodated in Sandringham House itself. It was Lady Diana's mother, Frances, who brought it into the Spencer family. Her father, Lord Fermoy, had been offered the tenancy by King George V, but when His

Lordship died shortly after his daughter's marriage to Viscount Althorp, the Spencers moved in. Diana was born there on 1 July, 1961, so she and her sisters, Jane and Sarah, grew up with the Royal Family as neighbours and with the Queen's youngest two children as companions.

When the engagement between the Prince of Wales and Lady Diana Spencer was announced, it caused a certain amount of surprise, because many of those in the royal circle had thought that Diana was closer to Prince Andrew, who is nearer her own age. In fact any one of Earl Spencer's three daughters could have been regarded as ideal for marrying into the Royal Family. They were all brought up in close proximity to the royals, so it was no mere pretence when Lord Spencer, asked if he thought his daughter would be nervous of marrying Prince Charles replied: 'Of course not. Why should she, we have all known the Royal Family for years.'

Diana herself was asked, before the marriage, if she ever felt uncomfortable in the presence of the Queen. She was surprised that the question should even be asked and replied: 'No, why should I be?' In fact there had never been a time in her short life when she had not known the Royal Family, so there was a natural and easy relationship between the Windsors and the Spencers.

Britain is world-famous for the pomp and pageantry of its traditional state ceremonial occasions, such as the State Opening of Parliament, in which the Prince and Princess play their part.

Diana as a young girl (right) with a Shetland pony; she rode as a child, but lost her nerve at about eight years old, after a bad fall in which she broke her arm. Now she prefers just to watch.

Diana's eldest sister, Lady Sarah, was an early girlfriend of Prince Charles and it was thought that she might become his wife. They had a brief relationship, but it was Sarah who finally turned him down in 1977, declaring, 'There never was a romance. He was the big brother I never had.' Three years later, just a month or so before that first date on board *Britannia*, Sarah married Neil McCorquodale, a former officer in the Coldstream Guards and the heir to a large printing fortune.

Earl Spencer's middle daughter, Lady Jane, is also married – and again there is a royal connection. Her husband is Sir Robert Fellowes, who is himself Private Secretary to the Queen and whose father was land agent at Sandringham. Lady Jane and her husband are now close neighbours of the Prince and Princess of Wales, as they occupy a delightful house within the Kensington Palace complex.

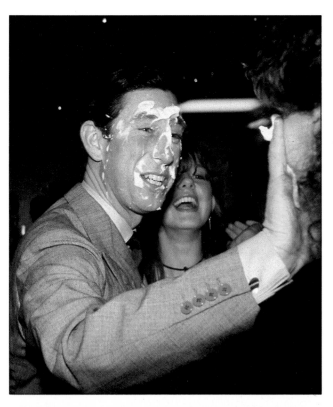

The Prince and Princess share a keen sense of humour. The Prince is well known for his love of 'Goonery', and he enjoys practical jokes: even a custard pie can't wipe the smile from the Prince's face! He has said: 'The most important thing a person in my position can have is a sense of humour ... being able to laugh at oneself.'

Returning to the early days of the royal romance, Prince Charles made his intentions pretty clear to Lady Diana in November 1980, when he gave her a personally conducted tour of his new home, Highgrove House in Gloucestershire, enthusiastically explaining his plans for its renovation. She was the first – and last – of his girlfriends to be afforded this privilege.

Both the Prince and the Princess enjoyed meeting Australian comedian Paul Hogan, who starred in the blockbuster movie *Crocodile Dundee.*

The Princess has met many women on the world stage, including America's first ladies Nancy Reagan (bottom) and Barbara Bush (right) and the British-born movie and TV star Joan Collins (below right).

Events moved swiftly after these first meetings and Prince Charles proposed to Lady Diana at dinner in his private suite within Buckingham Palace at the beginning of February 1980. This was on the eve of her departure for Australia, where she was going to visit her mother for three weeks. Prince Charles later explained why he had proposed before she left. 'I wanted to give her a chance to think about it – to think if it was all going to be too awful.' He had no need to worry on that score; as she said shortly before the wedding: 'I never had any doubts about it. It's what I always wanted.'

The official announcement of the engagement came at 11 o'clock on the morning of 24 February, 1981, and

Like her husband, seen here in his official gown as Doctor of Laws at Alberta University, the Princess began fulfilling public engagements when she was about twenty. Today they are both veterans.

was made by the late Lord Maclean, then Lord Chamberlain, to an audience of 200 people who were attending an investiture in the state ballroom at Buckingham Palace. The Archbishop of Canterbury was attending the General Synod of the Church of England and was speaking in a debate, somewhat appropriately, on marriage, when he interrupted the proceedings to tell the assembled delegates of the betrothal. The Prince and his fiancée met the press as an official couple for the first time and Diana proudly showed off her engagement ring – a large oval sapphire, surrounded by fourteen diamonds and set in white gold.

A little over a month later, on 27 March, 1981, the

Queen presided over a special meeting of the Privy Council at Buckingham Palace, to give her formal consent to the marriage of the Prince of Wales and Lady Diana Spencer. This was no mere ceremonial formality but a legal requirement under the Royal Marriages Act of 1772. This Act provides that any descendants, both male and female, of King George III's grandfather, George II, are required to obtain the consent of the sovereign, 'signified under the Great Seal, and declared in Council', before a marriage is contracted. Her Majesty uttered the single word 'approved' when she was presented with the proposal and afterwards posed for photographs with the happy couple. A little extra piece of history was also made on that day as it was the first and only time that photographs have been taken of the Privy Council.

As soon as Lady Diana became engaged to Prince Charles she was taken under the protection of the Royal Family and allocated a detective as a personal bodyguard. Prior to this she had been left to fend for herself against the hordes of reporters and photographers who had besieged her London flat. When she ventured out, she was followed by dozens of cameramen and microphone-wielding interviewers, with no help at all from the Royalty Protection Department, which guards all members of the Royal Family. Lady Diana handled her baptism of fire very well, especially when one considers that she had had no prior experience of dealing with the media. The Royal Family followed her progress and the Queen was heard to say: 'Well, she is going to have to learn to get used to this sort of thing. At least it's useful in that respect.'

However, from the moment of the official announcement it all changed: Lady Diana was taken under the wing of Buckingham Palace and the royal household and, from that day on, she would never even

be permitted to move beyond the confines of a royal residence without an armed police officer at her side.

She gave up her flat and moved into a suite of rooms at Buckingham Palace, not, as was commonly reported at the time, at Clarence House, home of Queen Elizabeth the Queen Mother, to whom her maternal grandmother, Ruth, Lady Fermoy has been a lady-in-waiting for many years. Lady Diana did, however, spend a great deal of the following months at Clarence House, where she was

Diana and her children love seaside holidays, when they can build sand castles on the beach, sunbathe and swim. Here they are with relatives over Easter, 1990, on holiday on Necker, tycoon Richard Branson's private Caribbean island.

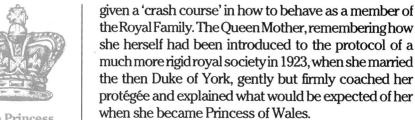

The Princess has matured since marriage and motherhood. Her public role and the affection of the crowds who turn out to greet her everywhere have given her great confidence. She loves people and, unlike Prince Charles, who enjoys solitude, is very gregarious. The popular Princess is presented with posies, and sometimes garlands, wherever she goes.

given a 'crash course' in how to behave as a member of the Royal Family. The Queen Mother, remembering how she herself had been introduced to the protocol of a much more rigid royal society in 1923, when she married the then Duke of York, gently but firmly coached her protégée and explained what would be expected of her when she became Princess of Wales.

There were of course certain similarities in their backgrounds. Both Lady Elizabeth Bowes-Lyon and Lady Diana Spencer came from long-established aristocratic families with centuries of royal association. Both their fathers had served the Crown and they had

both grown up knowing their future husbands from childhood. So there was nothing surprising about Lady Diana looking to the Queen Mother for guidance, nor in Her Majesty's obvious delight in her favourite grandson's choice of bride.

The period leading up to the marriage was an exciting but difficult time for the nineteen-year-old who just a few weeks earlier had been teaching infants at a kindergarten school in Pimlico. After the comparative freedom of living in her own flat, with three companions, and of coming and going as she pleased, she now had to adjust

From a shy teenager, Diana has blossomed into the biggest star the Royal Family has seen this century.

to living within the confines not only of a royal palace but also of both a rigid daily timetable and a calendar that was arranged for months, sometimes years, ahead. Across the road from Clarence House is St James's Palace, where the state ballroom was utilised as a rehearsal room for the royal wedding. The Assistant Private Secretary to the Prince of Wales, Oliver Everett, who is now the librarian at Windsor Castle, was brought in to put Lady Diana through her paces. The ballroom was divided into segments representing the exact dimensions of the high altar area in St Paul's Cathedral, where the ceremony was to take place. Chalk marks were made on the polished floor and squares of paper were laid out, showing the precise position of everyone of importance who would be at the wedding. Diana rehearsed over and over again, wearing a twenty-five-foot length of paper pinned to her dress to give her an idea of what it would be like when she wore the real wedding dress. All this so

that, by the time the actual service took place, she would know exactly where she had to stand, where everybody else would be and how many steps she had to take from A to B. It was an introduction to the sort of attention to detail that would become part of her everyday life from then on.

One of the Queen's ladies-in-waiting, Lady Susan Hussey, who has been in royal service for more than a quarter of a century and who was to become one of

Royal tours bring the Prince and Princess into contact with different peoples, cultures and customs. In the ten years since their marriage, they have visited Africa, America, the Middle East, the Far East, and Australasia.

Prince William's godmothers, instructed Lady Diana in the way she should behave in public. How, as a member of the Royal Family, she should be friendly but never allow familiarity. This was a little difficult for Diana, who is by nature an affectionate and outgoing person and has been described by some of her oldest friends as 'a toucher who would kiss the dustman if she felt like it'.

The arrangements for the wedding were left in the capable and experienced hands of the Lord Chamberlain, Lord Maclean, although traditionally the father of the bride both organises and pays for the wedding service and reception. The Queen, recognizing the difficulty in which this could place the parents of her sons' brides, has paid for the weddings of both the Prince of Wales and the Duke of York – a thoughtful and generous gesture that was greatly appreciated in both cases. It also meant of course that, although a wedding should be a purely private, family affair, this one was to be the most public of private events, because of the position held by the

bridegroom. In the event, the Queen only had to pay around £60,000 of the total costs of some £500,000. The country paid for the 3,500 police officers and 1,950 members of the armed forces who were on duty. Even so, Lord Spencer remarked afterwards, 'Thank God, I don't have to pay for it.'

The Lord Chamberlain issued a three-page ruling about wedding souvenirs, which were to be in good taste: neither the Royal Arms nor photographs of the

**Day or night, formally or informally dressed, the Princess makes heads
turn. She is admired everywhere for her beauty,
style and elegance.**

couple were to appear on tea towels or T-shirts. Undeterred, the souvenir industry sprang into instant activity, manufacturing over 2,000 items ranging from plastic thimbles to crystal goblets retailing at over £1,500 a set.

The Charles and Diana industry was eventually to be worth more than £20 million and it provided a welcome shot in the arm for factories and shops at a time when they were desperate for something to lift their depressed summer sales figures.

The press latched on to every aspect of the romance and when it was announced that a young husband and wife team, David and Elizabeth Emanuel, had been

Life is fun for the young princes, whether playing at firemen on an old-fashioned fire engine or competing at their school sports day.

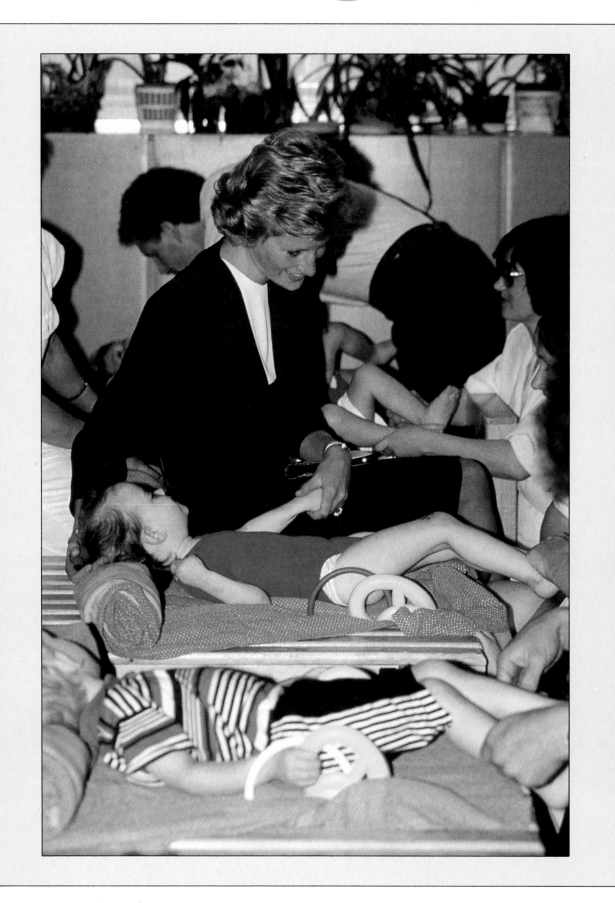

chosen to design and make the wedding dress, they became instant celebrities in their own right. Lady Diana's choice of the Emanuels was a complete break with the royal tradition of selecting a designer from the established fashion houses. It gave an indication that the future Princess of Wales was a young woman of independent spirit and tastes who would establish her own unique style in the years to come, although no one then could even have guessed at the impact she would actually have on the British fashion scene within a few short years. She has been described as a one-woman fashion industry. The British millinery trade, for instance, credits

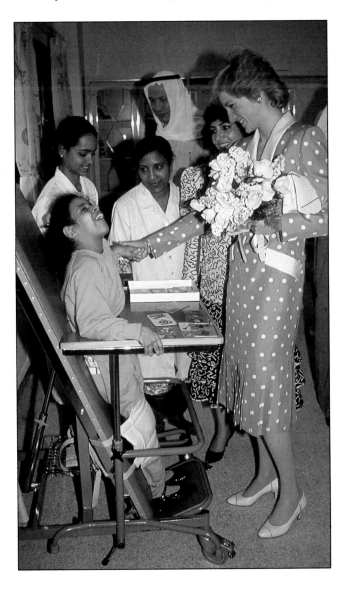

The Princess has a deeply-rooted sense of duty, but she also truly cares for others, especially children, as her genuine compassion for an American 'AIDS baby' (right) demonstrates.

Both the Prince and the Princess love going skiing. However, the Princess has made it clear that she does not like posing for press photographers while on private holidays.

her with being the sole reason behind young women wearing hats on almost any occasion these days, when, prior to the wedding, most women in their twenties wouldn't be seen dead in a hat.

During the run-up to the wedding, Lady Diana was given a gentle introduction to the royal round of public engagements. She accompanied the Queen and the Duke of Edinburgh to a garden party at Victoria Barracks, Windsor, attended a dedication service in the parish church at Tetbury, near her future home, and also watched her fiancé open a new operating theatre in the town's hospital. She was not required to say anything on these occasions and she was never permitted to attend any of the functions alone. It was simply a way of

showing her to the people and allowing her a glimpse of what was to come.

If Lady Diana had any doubts about her future role, she never showed them for an instant. For although she was accustomed to being in the presence of royalty, she was nevertheless a commoner and had not been brought up to live in the public glare. So it must have been quite a burden for such a young girl suddenly to find herself the centre of attention and to have not only to look her best at all times but also to smile and make small talk with people she had never met before, would probably never meet again and with whom she had little in common. However, whenever Lady Diana appeared in public, she seemed happy and relaxed – almost as if she had been doing it all her life.

The evening before the wedding there was a massive celebration in Hyde Park with a spectacular fireworks display watched by half a million people, including the Queen, the Duke of Edinburgh, Prince Charles and other members of the Royal Family, together with a number of other distinguished royal guests from overseas who had

The Princess has brought real glamour to the Royal Family. With her height and slender figure, she could be a top-flight model, were she not a future queen consort. However, few would have forecast that she would become such a glamorous world figure when she first came to the public notice ten years ago.

been invited to the wedding. It was the largest display of its kind in Britain for more than two centuries, but the bride was not present. If Lady Diana saw the fireworks at all, she must have watched them from a window in Clarence House, where she had moved for the night before the wedding, in keeping with the tradition that the bride and groom should not see each other from then until they meet in church.

July 29, 1981, was the royal wedding day and the occasion prompted the biggest media event the world had ever known. Seven hundred million would watch the proceedings as they were televised live by the BBC; a further 250 million would listen on the radio, while more than 50 million would watch recorded highlights later in the day. Altogether, the combined efforts of the media would reach a worldwide audience of over 1,000 million people in 141 countries.

Glamour on the beach: Diana's exotic leopard print outfit with its wrap skirt.

Two thousand six hundred guests arrived in St Paul's Cathedral – one of the reasons why it was chosen in preference to Westminster Abbey, the traditional royal wedding church, was that only 1,800 people could be seated in the Abbey. The guests included 160 presidents and prime ministers, most of the surviving European royals and all the close friends of the bride and groom. The Queen had also insisted on 200 places for members of her staff from Buckingham Palace, Sandringham and Balmoral. Lady Diana's three former flatmates sat

Holiday times bring relief from royal duties – and a chance to be buried in the sand by the children!

A cuddle for Prince Harry; the Princess's priorities are being a good wife and mother.

together in one of the best positions right at the front of the congregation. At this, the most important moment of her life, she was not about to forget her old friends.

The night before the wedding, tens of thousands of people had camped out along the processional route, anxious to secure the best vantage points. By six o'clock on the morning of 29 July, The Mall was already crowded with men, women and children standing five deep along the decorated thoroughfare.

At 10.37 a.m. precisely, Lady Diana Spencer left Clarence House with her father, Earl Spencer, in the Glass Coach, which has been used by all royal brides since King George V had it built for his coronation in 1910.

When on duty, whether walking over cloaks flung down for her à la Sir Walter Raleigh, making curtsies to foreign monarchs, such as her friend King Juan Carlos of Spain, or acting as a royal ambassadress at banquets abroad, the Princess shines.

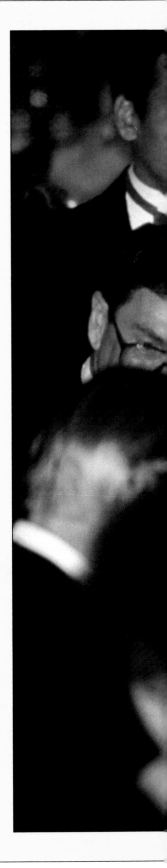

Just before the bride's procession left Clarence House, the Crown Equerry, Sir John Miller, confided to the Lord Chamberlain that he had a slight problem. Lady Diana wanted to exercise the bride's prerogative and arrive late at St Paul's. Sir John had been organising royal ceremonial transport for twenty-five years and never once had any of his carriages been unpunctual. It was a proud record and one that he was anxious to preserve. At the same time he did not want to upset the woman who would one day be Queen of England. Eventually a compromise was reached: the bride arrived at St Paul's just thirty seconds after the appointed time; the bride was satisfied and Sir John's timetable was barely disrupted.

Lady Diana looked radiantly beautiful and the ceremony went smoothly apart from one minor hiccup

when she got Prince Charles' names the wrong way round. She later explained: 'Well, with four names it's quite something to get organised.' It was a tiny human error that warmed the hearts of the millions watching and listening. Prince Charles also showed a few nerves when he made the promise, 'All thy worldly goods with thee I share.'

The wedding ring was fashioned by the royal jewellers, Collingwood's of Conduit Street, London, from a small nugget of pure 22-carat gold that was presented to the Queen Mother in 1923, when, as Lady Elizabeth Bowes-Lyon, she married the Duke of York (later King George VI). The gold came from the Clogau Mine in North Wales and was used for the wedding rings of the Queen (1948), Princess Margaret (1960) and Princess Anne (1973). There was even enough left over for the Duchess of York's wedding ring in 1987.

The wedding was conducted by the Archbishop of Canterbury and prayers were offered by the representatives of four different churches: by Lord Coggan, a former Archbishop of Canterbury, by the Roman Catholic Cardinal Hume, by the Moderator of the Church of Scotland and by the Rev Harry Williams, formerly Dean of Prince Charles' college in Cambridge and the first person to refer to the bride as 'Diana, Princess of Wales'.

The Speaker of the House of Commons, George Thomas (now Viscount Tonypandy), read the lesson and, while the wedding party was signing the registers (there were three in all – the Royal Marriage Register, which is kept in the custody of the Lord Chamberlain, plus two cathedral registers and the distinguished visitor's book), the New Zealand soprano Kiri te Kanawa sang an aria and chorus from *Samson*, a Handel oratorio.

The Princess has an innate sense of what suits her and has developed that into her own individual style. She loves bright, vibrant colours and sleek tailored lines. Exciting young designers whose talents she has brought to the fore include Arabella Pollen, Bruce Oldfield and Jasper Conran. The Princess has been credited with turning the British fashion industry into such a successful multi-million-pound business that London has all but eclipsed Paris and Rome as the fashion centre of the world.

After the signing of the registers, the Prince and Princess of Wales returned to the choir to be greeted by a fanfare, and this was followed by Elgar's *Pomp and Circumstance March No 4* as they proceeded back down the nave towards the door of the cathedral, where they were greeted by resounding cheers of welcome and congratulation from the waiting crowds. The subsequent wedding breakfast at Buckingham Palace was attended by only 120 of the 1,800 guests – the remainder had to make their own arrangements.

The Prince and Princess spent their wedding night at Broadlands, the home of Earl Mountbatten, where the Queen and Prince Philip had also spent part of their

As a toddler, William caused at least one security alert by inquisitively pressing an alarm button at home. 'William is just like me. Always in trouble,' says his mother. Although she has the help of nannies, the Princess has always taken a major hand in looking after the boys. 'It's tiring work looking after children,' she said once. 'I know because I have to look after my two boys and by Sunday I am a stretcher case.'

Prince William is very polite, but not at all shy. Indeed, like the hero of the *Just William* children's stories, he can be a little imp.

honeymoon. They then flew out to Gibraltar to join the Royal Yacht *Britannia* for a cruise in the Mediterranean. It was the first royal visit to Gibraltar since 1954 and the local people put on a tremendous display of patriotism. Nearly 500 small boats accompanied *Britannia* as she sailed out of the harbour with a band from the garrison playing Rod Stewart's hit of the day, 'Sailing', on the dockside. The Prince and Princess visited the Greek Isles, where they swam together in secluded coves, watched over by units of the Greek armed forces who were on duty to keep prying photographers away. The royal couple also paid a courtesy call on President Sadat of Egypt. Less than two months later, Prince Charles would return to Cairo to walk in the funeral procession of the assassinated Egyptian president.

Travel plays a large part even in the private lives of the royal couple. At weekends, they drive from London to their country house in Gloucestershire. The Prince and Princess are both keen motorists. Prince Charles likes Aston Martins and the Princess drives several cars, including a Jaguar XJS.

For Diana it was a taste of what was to become the norm in her future life. Even on their honeymoon, she and her husband were constantly on show and, in each country they visited, there were official functions to attend and formal presentations to be made. On board *Britannia*, the Princess made friends with some of the crew, even joining them on one occasion in their mess below decks where they were having a quiet drink in their off-duty hours. Of course, many of the young sailors were her age and she saw nothing wrong in socialising with them. It was gently but firmly pointed out to her that in her new position it simply would not do for her to fraternise so openly with people who were, after all, servants of the Crown, and she wisely took the hint. On subsequent voyages the Princess dined with the officers, but below decks was strictly out of bounds.

Following the cruise, the couple returned to Balmoral to plan for the hectic time ahead. For the Princess it would mean a new and demanding role. As well as playing her part in the 'Royal Firm' she also had the responsibility of settling into the new royal homes at Highgrove House and Kensington Palace. It was a decisive time for the young woman who had married the heir to the throne; the time when she started to establish her own unique personality and to set the style which was to become her personal trademark in the years to come.

The tour of Wales which followed the honeymoon was a triumph, Prince Charles readily acknowledging

For an audience with the Emir of Kuwait in March 1989, the Princess wore this pretty blue and white dress. She wore an outfit in the same cool colours for a 'picnic lunch' in Abu Dhabi.

that it was his wife that everyone wanted to see, not him. Her naturalness and her ability to talk to anyone from any age group are her greatest assets and within weeks she had assumed a place in the nation's affections that has not weakened at all during the ten years that she has been Princess of Wales.

It had been nearly eighty years since there was last a Princess of Wales and the people of the principality were determined that she would remember the welcome

The Princess is a country girl who prefers life in London, unlike Prince Charles, who was born there. For casual wear in the country, the Princess usually avoids traditional tweeds and sensible brogues, preferring a cricket sweater and jacket, something warm slipped over a dress, or trousers and a sloppy joe.

that they had prepared for her in the hillsides and valleys.

Her Royal Highness earned the immediate and spontaneous affection of the crowds when she emerged from the royal train at Caernarvon wearing an outfit of red and green – the national colours of Wales. It was on this occasion that the custom of giving her bouquets of flowers began. Prior to this no one would have dared to offer anything to a member of the Royal Family that had not been agreed beforehand. The Princess was delighted and her pleasure was reflected in the smiles she saw all around her.

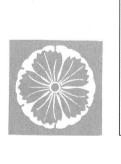

The Prince tends to keep to tailored, short-sleeved shirts and
immaculately-pressed slacks for casual wear. However, here is the
evidence that he does own a pair of jeans!

Royal 'walkabouts' have now become a familiar and expected part of any public engagement, but in 1981 they were still something of a rarity and they had never achieved the sort of informality that they did with the Princess of Wales. She accepted flowers and presents; one man even kissed her hand – after asking her permission, which was smilingly given.

The tour lasted three days and took in every part of Wales in a 400-mile journey that reached its climax in Cardiff, the capital city. In the City Hall the Princess, wearing a blue chiffon dress, was sworn in as the 53rd Freeman of the City – becoming only the second woman

to have been so honoured. To the delight and surprise of everyone present she made her speech of reply in Welsh, having learnt it, phonetically, in secret some weeks earlier. When she said she was proud to be Princess of Wales and 'would love to come again' she received a standing ovation. Prince Charles realized that he had a princess to be proud of and a wife whose charm and beauty would enable her to stand beside him on equal terms in any circumstances.

The first year of their marriage proved that the initial glow of public interest, which had begun with their engagement and reached a peak with their wedding, was

Both Charles and Diana hold top positions in the services. This allows the Princess to try her hand at driving tanks and the Prince to wear many different uniforms.

now to be fanned to white heat. They were never out of the news. Diana 'lookalikes' appeared in every town and village and even Prince Charles was moved to mention that he thought there was a little 'overkill' in the 'Diana mania' and girls should try to 'be themselves not clones of someone else.'

However, the Princess of Wales could do no wrong in the eyes of the public and when it was announced from Buckingham Palace that she was expecting her first baby, who would be christened before the first anniversary of the wedding, it set the seal on a year of the most intense royal interest since the Coronation in 1953.

Buckingham Palace announced that the Princess of Wales was pregnant for the first time on 5 November, 1981. The general assumption was that the royal baby – he would be second in line of succession to the throne – would be born in one of the royal residences, presumably in Buckingham Palace, as his father had been. However, the Princess showed what sort of parent she intended to become by insisting that her child should be born in hospital – in the Lindo Wing of St Mary's in Paddington (where both of Princess Anne's children were born), under the personal supervision of the Queen's gynaecologist, Mr George Pinker. It was the

first time that an heir presumptive would be delivered outside the privacy of a royal home.

When the time came for the baby's arrival, Prince Charles demonstrated that he too could adapt to modern ideas by accompanying his wife into the delivery room and remaining there throughout the birth. It was another 'first' for the royal couple. When Prince Charles himself was born in 1948, his father had stayed outside his wife's bedroom until summoned by a nurse once the baby had been safely delivered and mother and child were prepared to receive visitors.

Prince Charles has also claimed that when his children (the couple's second son, Prince Henry, was born in 1984) were very small, he liked to share their bath time occasionally, though he apparently drew the line at changing nappies.

The Princess has taken the children on holiday (top) without their father, who prefers active holidays. However, he does join them and the family of King Juan Carlos and Queen Sofia of Spain for seaside holidays in Majorca.

It was shortly after the birth of Prince William that rumours of tension in the marriage began circulating. There were several highly publicised arguments between the Prince and Princess both in the shooting field and on the ski slopes of Europe. The trouble was that these inevitably took place in front of platoons of press photographers and reporters who dogged the couple's footsteps waiting for exactly this to happen. Also around this time, a number of former royal servants began

The simplest of pale pink, wide-brimmed straw hats keeps the Princess
looking cool and elegant on a visit to Cameroon in 1990.

Pink is a favourite colour for the ultra-feminine Princess; she loves all shades from palest candyfloss to deepest fuchsia and wears it often. Diana is said to spend hundreds of thousands of pounds every year on clothes; her walk-in wardrobe fills two rooms at Kensington Palace.

Pink with red (right) was a daring fashion mix, but it worked in this stunning outfit, by two of Diana's top designers, Catherine Walker and milliner Philip Somerville.

offering titbits of gossip to the media about the private rows in Kensington Palace.

With any ordinary couple such disagreements would have been kept within the family; when the principals involved also happen to be the most newsworthy couple in the world, the most minor arguments can be elevated to major rows and rumours of a possible break-up in the marriage began to reach mammoth proportions.

It was all symptomatic of the strains involved behind the scenes in introducing a new, young and totally inexperienced member into the Royal Family and in maintaining her public image.

Part of the problem was that Diana had become so completely identified with the younger generation of women that they copied her every move. If she wore a dress or a piece of jewellery in a particular style, it immediately became *de rigueur* for thousands of other young women to do the same. The 'Diana look' was the most popular style in the Western world and her manners and behaviour were also slavishly followed.

Modern youngsters in Britain, Australia and the USA were also used to a freedom their mothers had never known, so when Diana 'kicked over the traces' in public, they were overjoyed. It was precisely the way they

wanted their heroine to behave, because it was the way they behaved themselves. The Princess became even more popular with the 'Diana groupies' when she rowed in public than she had been in the very early days when she was thought of as a 'Miss Goody Two-Shoes' who never said anything out of place or acted in the least bit outrageously.

Royal 'experts' have now written millions of words about the relationship between the Prince and Princess of Wales and the influence they have had on each other. Prince Charles is an intelligent and patient husband who has weathered the early storms with his younger wife; he is old enough and shrewd enough to be able to guide her in her public role, without appearing to dominate her. His influence does not appear obvious to the outsider, but those who know the couple well say he is a much more caring and guiding husband than he is given credit for.

The Princess of Wales has influenced her husband in a much more dramatic fashion. She has never made a secret of the fact that she does not care for field sports,

In Africa, the royal couple met traditional dancers (right) and a natty gentleman in tribal dress and a top hat (above).

**The Prince of Wales has always liked hazardous sports,
and polo is definitely dangerous.**

shooting and hunting in particular, and she is not prepared to compromise her principles either by taking part in these activities or by watching her husband kill animals for sport. As a child she was taught to ride, but an early fall caused her to lose her nerve and she has only recently been seen in the saddle once again: more, one suspects, as a gesture to the Queen, who loves to ride, than because the Princess herself has rediscovered such pleasures. Her dislike of shooting and hunting has actually caused Prince Charles to cut down on his days in the

The Princess is happy to be on the sidelines, supporting her husband and his team, and she turned out to watch him even when she was pregnant. After games are over, the Princess often presents the prizes, sometimes getting the chance to give her husband a congratulatory kiss.

field. He still likes to shoot at Sandringham with his father and he hunts with a local Gloucestershire pack when he can, but these days he does not spend nearly as much time on such activities as he once did, and this is due entirely to the influence of his wife.

However, the Princess does enjoy watching her husband play polo, which has become his passion in life. At least it was until a serious accident on the polo field in the summer of 1990 left him with his right arm broken in several places. Months later he was still in great pain, which necessitated a number of operations on his damaged limb. Throughout his three-hour ordeal in the operating theatre, the Princess remained in a room close by, until she was sure that he would recover. It was an example of the closeness that has developed between them over the years, in spite of the frequent separations and the consequent rumours about a coolness in their relationship.

Another way in which the Princess has influenced her husband is in his diet. Before she came into his life, Prince Charles loved to eat all the things he shouldn't: stodgy puddings, lots of potatoes and gooey desserts – nursery food. Her Royal Highness has changed all that. Today the Prince is to all intents and purposes a vegetarian, with red meat almost completely absent from the royal table. Although Prince Charles likes to claim that he was the one who began the move towards vegetarianism in the family, old friends of the Princess say it was she who persuaded him; she has always preferred dishes without meat.

Perhaps the most obvious way, at least to the outsider, in which the Princess has influenced her husband is in the way he dresses. Apart from his choice of jazzy, vividly striped shirts, which he has always chosen himself, his style was strictly low-key. For longer then he cares to remember, Prince Charles wore the same style of suit: a classic, two-button, single-breasted jacket with narrow lapels and two side-vents and trousers that were plain and narrow, with no turn-ups.

The Princess of Wales has changed all this. First of all she persuaded him to move his custom from his traditional tailor to a younger and infinitely more stylish firm, Anderson and Sheppard, in Savile Row. Now, for his everyday wear, the Prince of Wales wears fashionable, double-breasted suits with much wider lapels and buttonholes. The shoulders are more heavily padded than they used to be and the jackets are slightly 'waisted'

– but only slightly, at his own insistence. He still prefers the English look to the tighter and more figure-hugging continental style. The trousers of his suits and those he wears with casual jackets are now nearly all made with turn-ups and with pleats at the front. He is not particularly keen on them himself, but as he explained: 'I do it to please my wife.' However, the Prince of Wales is still rarely seen in a pair of jeans – although his wife often wears hers. This is one fashion Charles is still resisting and even the charms of his stylish and glamorous wife are barely enough to persuade him to be seen in public wearing this universal uniform of the trendy younger generation.

The Prince's collection of ties – comprising several hundred – includes those of all the regiments, colleges and organisations with which he is associated, and also a large number of vivid silk ties, each one chosen by the Princess.

The Princess collapses in giggles either when she finds something irresistibly funny or when she is nervous. Part of her appeal is that she still allows her natural feelings and reactions to show.

Below left: Prince William and Prince Harry ride with their father. One day they may play polo too, although the sport has its hazards. In June 1990, Prince Charles broke his right arm in a serious fall at Cirencester. When he left hospital after the first operation on the arm, the Princess was there to meet him.

Prince Charles will do almost anything to please his wife but he does dislike the very informal sports clothes she favours. He has always worn the same short-sleeved, but obviously tailored, shirts and immaculately pressed slacks that he still wears today, refusing absolutely to have anything to do with some of the more outlandish outfits his wife would like to see him in. She has, however, partially won the battle over his shoes. In the main, Prince Charles' shoes are still of the 'sensible' type that he wore at school and in the forces: black lace-ups with toecaps. Nevertheless, the Princess has managed to persuade her husband to try a few pairs of slip-on casuals, which he found he actually liked once he had become used to them. And he is now seen in public wearing them, to the obvious delight of his wife – and the British shoe industry!

The slender, elegant and very stylish Princess of Wales, on the other hand, became a leader of British fashion almost from the day she became a member of the Royal Family. Princess Diana has dressed her part perfectly and, in so doing, has set new standards in royal style. She has an innate sense of what suits her, even as regards innovative and adventurous styles, so that she can wear what might appear outrageous on other women, but it will look just right on her.

Before the Princess of Wales came on the scene, royal ladies were expected to be models of decorum. The younger royals, such as Princess Anne and the Duchess of Kent, tried to follow fashion, but they were never regarded as trend-setters themselves. Conventionality was the norm and the men and women who designed clothes for them knew that they must always play safe. It was a system that had remained unchanged since the early days of the century and no one was prepared to step out of line – until Diana

The Prince and Princess have sailed in everything from the Royal Yacht *Britannia* to a Maori war canoe. In Venice, in 1985, they took a brief but romantic trip in a gondola.

appeared. She not only knows instinctively what suits her from among the current fashions, but, more importantly, she knows how to adapt outfits both to her own personality and to the needs of the job. Whatever she wears in public has to be suitable for getting into and out of cars and aeroplanes, and as the Princess needs to appear as fresh at the end of a long and tiring day as she does first thing in the morning, everything has to be crease resistant.

Her choice of clothes has brought the talents of such designers as Arabella Pollen, Bruce Oldfield and Jasper Conran to the fore. These are young, exciting designers who know they can get the Princess to try almost

anything and, when she wears one of their outfits to a function, it generates the sort of publicity money alone cannot buy.

The Princess has been credited with turning the British fashion industry into a successful multi-million-pound international business so that London has all but

The Royal Family are tightknit and gather around the Queen at Christmas, New Year and Easter and to spend part of the summer holidays at Balmoral in Scotland. The whole family also celebrates the Queen Mother's birthdays.

The Queen has known Diana since the Princess was a child, when she
and her family lived in Park House, a grace-and-favour residence on the
royal estate at Sandringham.

eclipsed Paris and Rome as the fashion centre of the world. Yet she has said, 'clothes are not my priority. I enjoy bright colours and my husband likes to see me looking smart and presentable, but fashion isn't my big thing at all.' Hardly the words expected of a woman who is said to spend hundreds of thousands of pounds every year on a variety of day wear, evening dresses, ball gowns, casual clothes and sports equipment, who is said to possess two hundred pairs of shoes and three hundred pairs of earrings and whose wardrobe fills two full-size rooms at Kensington Palace.

To many people in the trade, the Princess constitutes a one-woman fashion industry. She has been acclaimed as the best-dressed woman in the world and, no matter what she might say herself, she was certainly the number one style-setter in Britain in the eighties and looks as if she will carry on that trend well into the nineties.

Although the Princess is quintessentially feminine, she has a boyish figure which allows her to wear masculine styles to devastating effect. Most of her leisure clothes fall into this category. Her height – 5 foot 10 inches – and slimness mean she can wear pencil-slim garments and show them off to their best advantage. She is slimmer now than when she married and wears a size 10 or 12 depending on the maker.

Champagne, kisses and dancing: it's all part of life on and off duty for the royal couple. However, the fun-loving Princess doesn't actually like champagne; and the Prince's heart sinks when he has to be first on the dance floor, but playing the game is part of the many duties they fulfil for their country. The kissing, of course, is private fun.

Diana was not widely-travelled when she married, but has since flown round the world with Charles. Wherever they go, they act as ambassadors for Britain. Whether they greet VIPs, listen to or make speeches, or take part in a version of the Japanese tea ceremony, their visits increase goodwill and often boost trade

The only articles in her wardrobe which are never worn are her fur coats. She possesses several but they are all stored in refrigerated chambers, as are the Queen's, in deference to the animal conservation movement. Even the headband the Princess wears as part of her skiing outfit is fake fur: the only item she wears that is not the real thing.

The Princess of Wales has shown how she can wear stylish clothes that are also practical and suitable for her role. Hers is a unique wardrobe, put together with but one purpose in mind: to ensure that Her Royal Highness can carry out her duties in a manner that will show the Royal Family in the best possible light. By wearing the cream of British products, she also acts as a travelling showcase for an important national industry that fully recognises the unbeatable role model they have in her.

The Charles and Diana 'set' has been described as 'the new court' though this is a description guaranteed to send the Prince of Wales into an instant rage. He will hear no talk of setting up a separate establishment in competition with Buckingham Palace. The idea of abdication is of course a nonstarter. The Queen accepts her role as a sacred trust to which she is committed for life and, when she was anointed with holy oil at her

coronation in Westminster Abbey in 1953, the religious aspect of the ceremony was real to her in every sense. There is no question of her 'opting out' in favour of her son. Indeed, he would be the last person in the world to wish for such an occurrence. He knows full well that it may be many years yet before he becomes king, but the role of 'king-in-waiting' is one he has come to terms with and he wants nothing more than that his mother should reign until the twenty-first century.

When he and the Princess of Wales moved their offices from Buckingham Palace to St James's Palace, it caused a certain amount of comment and raised eyebrows at the time. The Lord Chamberlain and his staff, who occupied the rooms now used by Prince Charles and his household, did not want to move. Why should they? They had the use of the best accommodation in any of the royal residences – and if they were slightly away from the rest of the royal household, was that entirely a bad thing? Visiting their offices at St James's Palace was a bit like visiting a private club and the accommodation was far superior to the more cramped offices across the road in Buckingham Palace.

It was for this very reason that the Prince of Wales decided to make the move. He and his large staff (second

Abroad, the Princess flies the flag by almost always wearing British fashions. Although quintessentially feminine, Diana can wear masculine styles, such as bow ties, to devastating effect. After dark the Princess dazzles in fabulous gowns, such as the black and white creation (centre right). She has worn the smart black veiled hat (below left) at remembrance ceremonies.

only to that of the Queen herself) were working in a corner of Buckingham Palace that meant any visitor had to travel along what appeared to be miles of corridors before reaching the Wales' suite on the ground floor. The obvious solution – to the Prince at any rate – was that he should move to St James's Palace and the Lord Chamberlain should move to Buckingham Palace. A feeble rearguard action was fought but the battle was lost before it had really begun. Prince Charles wanted to move; it made good sense to him – and the Queen agreed.

The offices of the Prince and Princess of Wales are now located in what used to be the home of Prince Henry, Duke of Gloucester. They are large, elegant and beautifully decorated rooms, with crystal chandeliers and a superb collection of oil paintings. The only slight jar is the constant hum of computers from the main

The young princes have quite different characters: Prince Harry is quieter than Prince William. Even so, the Princess always buys two of everything, so there are no squabbles.

office. The location also poses security problems for the Royalty Protection Department, which has the responsibility of guarding all members of the Royal Family. Prince Charles' personal office is situated on the first floor of St James's Palace, looking out onto a public road. As a self-confessed fresh air fanatic, His Royal Highness insists on having the picture windows wide open at all times, which makes it possible to see him clearly from the street below. The problems for the security men are obvious – but making Prince Charles see their point of view is another matter altogether.

It is here that all manner of people come to meet the Prince and Princess of Wales. Almost every day the Court Circular, which lists the engagements and visitors of the Royal Family, will show that a large number of people have been 'received by the Prince and Princess of Wales'. These people could range from the commanding officers of service units associated with Their Royal

Toppers and picture hats for a day at the races. The Princess of Wales invariably wins the fashion stakes, and always stands out in a crowd.

Polo has played a major part in Prince Charles' life, as it did in that of his father, Prince Philip, and of his great-uncle, Lord Mountbatten.

Polo obviously brings out the Prince's chivalrous nature, as pictures of him kissing his mother's hand (left) and showing tenderness towards his then pregnant wife prove.

Highnesses, who arrive to be formally presented when either taking up their appointments or making their farewells, to leaders of Commonwealth countries who personally brief the Prince on matters concerning their particular country. Others who are summoned to the royal presence include businessmen, social workers, artists and politicians, all with one purpose in mind: to keep the Prince and Princess fully informed on the widest variety of issues. Each visitor has his or her own place in the royal scheme of things and, when the day comes that Prince Charles ascends the throne, he and his wife will surely be the most widely informed couple

the British monarchy has ever known. This is in part what has given rise to the claims that there is a separate court, but the Queen is fully aware of what is taking place in St James's Palace and she has gladly given her approval to the way in which her eldest son is preparing for the day when he will succeed her.

Another way in which the Prince and Princess of Wales use their partnership to enlarge their knowledge of world affairs is through their entertaining. A large number of distinguished men and women have been delighted and surprised to receive an invitation to Kensington Palace. They soon find out that this is not

If Prince Charles' team wins and Princess Diana is presenting the prizes, a congratulatory kiss is in order!

Hats had gone out of fashion until the Princess of Wales brought them back into vogue.

entirely due either to their scintillating personalities or to their sparkling dinner-table repartee. Lunches and dinners held by the Prince and Princess of Wales nearly always have a purpose: there is always something the guests can do either for Prince Charles or for his wife; though in all fairness, this is never for them personally, but for one of their causes.

Show business stars such as Placido Domingo and Dame Kiri te Kanawa have dined at Kensington Palace

Hats give Diana confidence and, whether she is sporting a natty little pillbox or one of her famous wide-brimmed creations, she invariably looks a treat. She had expert help at the start from her mother's milliner, John Boyd, but today her top milliner is Philip Somerville.

only to find afterwards that they are persuaded either literally to 'sing for their supper', or to perform at a charity function which will benefit one of the Wales' organisations.

Even Margaret Thatcher found that there is no such thing as a free lunch where the Prince and Princess are concerned. When Prime Minister, she was frequently a guest only to find that her influence was needed in a particular quarter. However, no one seems to object to being manipulated in this way. This is probably because the Prince and Princess themselves give so much of their own precious time and energy to these various causes, so there's nothing selfish in this exploitation.

One of the most generous sectors of the British population is the Asian community. Many Asians have become very successful and extremely rich businessmen and the Prince of Wales has not been slow in involving them in his pet projects. At a recent dinner in Kensington Palace all the guests were Asian multimillionaires. The Prince was looking for donations for the Prince's Trust, one of his favourite charities. As the guests departed after a convivial evening they left behind cheques for amounts ranging between £25,000 and £100,000. They knew when they accepted the royal invitation that there was going to be a price to pay – and they were delighted to be associated with a project headed by the future king.

Intense scrutiny of the royal marriage has become a massive spectator sport with every reader and viewer an expert on the subject. Of course nobody will ever know what really goes on, or indeed has gone on, in the privacy

In Indonesia in 1989, Prince Charles reached to touch a special statue of Buddha in the world's oldest Buddhist temple and the Princess tried her hand at bowls while visiting a leprosy hospital near Jakarta.

In 1989, the royal couple gazed out from the balcony of a house (left) in a replica of a local Indonesian village. In Thailand in 1988 they visited the Temple of the Emerald Buddha (below). In 1990 Prince Charles stood on a suspension bridge (below left) built in Cameroon by Operation Raleigh.

of the marriage of the Prince and Princess of Wales. How could they? The Wales' private life is just that, so that all we have to go on is such circumstantial evidence as is publicly available.

So called 'royal experts' have built up a picture out of the millions of words and thousands of photographs that have appeared in the past ten years and the occasional glimpse of the attitudes of the principals themselves has provided a few clues.

In the beginning, Charles was an anxious, introspective fiancé and husband and Diana an exuberant and largely uneducated royal bride who confessed to being 'as thick as a plank'. Ten years later, Charles has become much more of an extrovert, even if he still displays the odd anxiety, while Diana has blossomed into the biggest star the Royal Family has seen this century.

Charles took a husband's pride in his beautiful and glamorous young wife, being only slightly put out if her presence prevented people from paying attention to him and the more serious issues on which he wanted to air his views.

What has become more apparent in recent years is the way in which they have each adapted their lives to accommodate the other while at the same time maintaining their own individual interests. As Prince Charles pursues his ambitions to improve architecture, the state of the English language and the environment through his public speeches and the making of films for

Much of the Princess's life is scheduled months ahead, so the times when she can wind down and relax with her children are very precious.

television, his wife shows her compassion for some of the worst contemporary problems. Princess Diana heads the charity Turning Point, which is one of the least glamorous of any organisation associated with a member of the Royal Family. It looks after young men and women suffering from the effects of drink and drug abuse. Many of them do not want to be helped and may even despise those who are trying to do so. Before the Princess of Wales came on the scene, Turning Point had great difficulty in attracting the attention of the British public and, more importantly, they were unable to get any influential fund-raisers on their side. Diana made all the

The Queen and other members of her family, who are used to wet holidays in Scotland, don't seem to mind the rain; according to the Princess, Prince Charles loves it. However, although Diana would rather have sunshine, nothing can dampen her spirits on a public engagement. Even if the heavens do open.

difference. Once she had become their patron and appeared at one or two of their events, everything changed. All of a sudden the rich and powerful found a new cause to support and Turning Point is now one of the success stories of the last five years.

Prince Charles is delighted at his wife's involvement, saying, 'As Diana begins to do various things, she will meet more people and develop her own style.' A perfect example of the way this has happened was demonstrated in a speech she made in 1989 at the Barnardo's annual conference. She wrote it herself and delivered it with confidence, wit and compassion. The result was a new Diana: a more serious woman than ever before and one

Whether travelling to the Ceremony of the Garter (right) or Trooping the Colour (left), Diana looks good in her favourite colour, pink.

Above and above centre: after Trooping the Colour, the Royal Family watch an RAF fly-past from a balcony at Buckingham Palace.

who matches her husband in her efforts to improve the lot of those less fortunate than herself.

This is one of the ways in which the Prince and Princess are totally united. They are both deeply concerned with the problems of those people who do not seem to have much in life. The pop star and famine relief worker *extraordinaire*, Bob Geldof, once summed them up, saying, 'How ironic that royalty should turn out to be the common man.'

The Princess has a natural ability to talk to people of all ages and from all walks of life; she does it brilliantly and with no apparent effort. She is unselfconscious when she visits children in hospital or the elderly in old people's homes. They seem to relate to her in a way they find impossible with any other royal lady. When she visited the Princess of Wales hospital in Bridgend, Mid

Glamorgan, in February 1990, she faced a daunting line-up of civic dignitaries waiting to greet her. She was pleasant and courteous to everyone she met, and then, right at the end of the line, waiting to be presented, was Viscount Tonypandy, George Thomas, the former Speaker of the House of Commons. He had only recently been released from hospital himself after treatment for throat cancer and, when the Princess saw him, she threw her arms around him and kissed him saying, 'George, how wonderful to see you looking so well.' All formality was forgotten and the tone was set for the rest of the visit.

Later, in a ward of the hospital, she sat on the bed of one elderly patient who told her she was 'as pretty as the Queen Mother'. She blushed and replied, 'I bet you say that to all the girls.' Prince Charles is also one of the world's great communicators, being able to converse easily with youngsters from deprived inner-city ghettos or with farm labourers working in the Duchy of Cornwall's fields, and making them feel that what they have to say is worth listening to. In his case, however, this ability has come through years of training rather than as the result of a natural talent. He is not naturally comfortable in crowds and prefers solitude to the company of others. Where the Princess is gregarious by nature, he is reserved. The weight of his position has always sat heavily on his shoulders and, from an early age, he has been made

Above: a tender royal moment. Right and above right: blue jeans were not common royal casual wear before the advent of the Princess, but she often wears them to horsy events.

Although Prince Charles does own a pair of jeans, he's usually seen off duty in jodhpurs, corduroys or slacks.

aware that he is different from other men and that, consequently, others must be kept at a distance. It has not made for a comfortable existence, but it is the only one he has ever known, and he has become used to it, without either wishing for change, or even knowing that such a possibility exists.

Diana loves people; when she is introduced to someone, her natural reaction is to like them until they give her cause to change her opinion. Charles' initial reaction to strangers is one of slight suspicion. In his case trust has to be earned; he has taken years to build up the inner circle of friends and advisers who give him the only taste of the outside world he is permitted to have. Diana, however, has retained some, but not all, of the friendships that she made at school and when she first came to live in London. Part of her royal induction has been knowing which of her acquaintances she could encourage and which needed to be 'dropped' as she moved further and further into the public eye.

Both the Prince and Princess adore family life, though for different reasons. He does so because, in spite of being separated from his parents on many occasions as a child, he has always felt secure in their love and support. She does so because her own parents' marriage broke up when she was at an impressionable age and she has been determined ever since that her own children

The Princess, whose parents divorced when she was a child, is committed to her own family life, and helps others through her work for RELATE.

will never suffer through not being able to count on both mother and father being there when they are needed.

When William and Henry were very small, Prince Charles gave up a number of official engagements in order to be with them, and this attracted a certain amount of criticism. It was claimed that, as a senior member of the Royal Family, duty should come before family. Clearly, Prince Charles has never neglected his public duties, but he obviously felt that his wife and children needed him more than anyone else at the time – and the public seemed to agree. When it was revealed that he had cut down on the number of engagements just to be at home more often, a survey in a national newspaper showed that the majority of people in Britain thoroughly approved of his actions as a young married

The Princess's walk-in wardrobes are filled with ravishing garments from the pick of British fashion designers. Many of her most glamorous numbers for day and evening wear are in eye-catching red or pink. They enhance the 'star quality' that has made her one of the world's most photographed women.

man. In the enlightened atmosphere of the eighties, it was what most young wives would want their husbands to do if it were possible and the sympathy which went out to the Prince and Princess showed again that they had got it right by trying to keep in touch with some of the realities of life.

On the general question of their children's upbringing, the Prince and Princess have few disagreements. They both felt it was vital for the children to be kept as close to them as possible when they were very young, which is why both William and Henry went to nursery and day

The royal couple enjoy skiing and Prince Charles takes an annual winter sports holiday at Klosters. The Princess's enthusiasm waned after the 1988 tragedy in which Major Hugh Lindsay lost his life.

school near Kensington Palace. The Princess of Wales was able to take them to school herself most mornings, and both she and the Prince were at home in the evenings to listen to the boys' accounts of their day.

If the Prince and Princess are abroad without their children, they will telephone every day. The boys love to hear from their parents and, in the case of the Princess, it helps to keep her from getting too homesick on an extended tour. Prince Charles also likes to chat on the telephone with his sons but, as he grew up in an environment in which it was perfectly normal for his own parents to be absent for long periods, he hasn't quite come to terms with his wife's preoccupation with the children.

Home during the week is an apartment, or rather two apartments combined into one rather large residence: Number 9 and Number 10 Kensington Palace. There are twenty-five principal rooms; even so it is not the largest home in the palace: that distinction goes to the Gloucesters', who have thirty-five rooms. The house in which the Prince and Princess of Wales live was badly damaged by bombs during the Second World War and the repairs and renovations took five years to complete after the war. Their immediate next-door neighbours are Prince and Princess Michael of Kent, with whom they share a walled courtyard as a parking area for their cars.

The whole of Kensington Palace has been divided into grace-and-favour apartments for members of the Royal Family and the household. At one time so many elderly royal ladies lived there that Prince Philip dubbed it 'The Aunt Heap'.

The Wales' house is L-shaped and on three floors and its interior gives the impression of being that of a typical English country mansion. The entrance hall is large, light and airy and is dominated by a green and grey carpet inlaid with the motif of the Prince of Wales feathers. It is not particularly pleasing to look at and even the Prince himself has been known to remark on its 'garish' appearance.

On the ground floor is the 'throne room' – the gentlemen's lavatory. This is decorated with Prince Charles' personal collection of vintage, mahogany

The royal couple are respected and welcomed all around the world. On the Riviera for the 1987 Cannes Film Festival, the Princess appeared in a puffball dress (left), which she wore for a visit to the town hall.

lavatory seats, in which he takes great pride; as he also does in the unique collection of newspaper cartoons – all originals – which graces the cloakroom next door. As one ascends the magnificent Georgian staircase, which was badly damaged in the war but is now restored to its former glory, the eye is caught by a large painting of the Princess of Wales. The artist was John Ward and the painting shows her Royal Highness in her wedding dress.

Prince William and Prince Harry are their parents' pride and joy.

Prince Charles loves this portrait, which was commissioned by him when he learned that his wife was expecting their second child.

On the first floor, the drawing room is warm and inviting, with pale yellow walls and deep armchairs and sofas covered in a light peach coloured fabric. This is the room where the Prince and Princess usually greet their guests, who often gather round the full-size Broadwood grand piano. Guests such as Elton John have played this piano, but the Princess, although no mean performer herself, prefers to play for her own pleasure rather than in front of an audience. Dinner parties are held in the

At Wetherby School sports day in 1988, Prince Charles competed against the other fathers and the Princess sprinted barefoot to the finishing tape, to beat the other mothers. However, she was beaten herself the following two years.

Diana isn't the only member of
the family who is ahead of the
field when it comes to hats.
Prince Charles has a fair
selection of headgear, too.

main dining room where sixteen can be comfortably seated around the circular mahogany table. Both the Prince and Princess like the idea of a round table as it gives them a good view of all their guests, and no one is offended by being placed at the foot of the table.

The Princess of Wales also has a sitting room, which is very much her own domain. The wall coverings were made to her order and were designed by the young South African interior designer Dudley Poplak, who also did part of Highgrove House. At Kensington Palace the sitting room decoration includes the Prince of Wales feathers in the pattern. The room which is used more than any other by Prince Charles is his study, situated on the first floor. Papers and books cover almost every available surface and nobody, wife or servant, would dare move a thing. The Prince has a hand-written note on his desk saying: 'Do not move anything. They are where they are because I want them there.' There is a large collection of family photographs in the study with pride of place going to one of his great-uncle, the late Earl

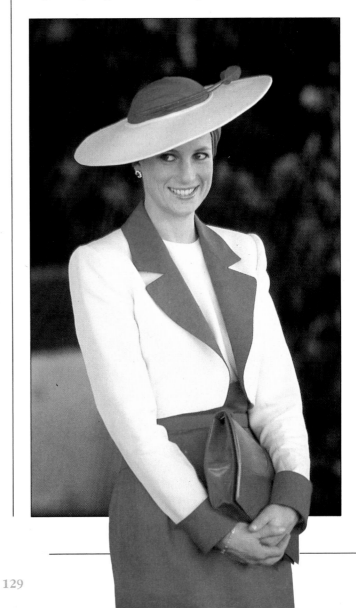

The Prince and Princess of Wales met the Pope at the Vatican during the royal couple's tour of Italy in 1985. Keeping to traditional custom for a papal audience, the Princess wore a black dress and veil.

Mountbatten of Burma. One unusual item is the Polish Solidarity flag which stands on the window sill. The room is soundproofed, which is just as well because this is where Prince Charles likes to sit late at night playing records of his favourite operas on his stereo, with the volume turned up high.

The main bedroom suite is also on the first floor with the master bedroom alone covering an area forty-five feet square. The bed is a massive four-poster which

Prince Charles may have a walk in mind, but his pet dog, Tigger (below), looks as if he would prefer to be driven in the Prince's Aston Martin (right).

The Princess also loves cars (left) and experts say she is an excellent driver, even if she does like driving too fast: she has been warned a couple of times about speeding.

Prince Charles brought with him from Buckingham Palace when he was married. It is of truly gigantic proportions, being 7ft 6ins wide. One luxury the Prince and Princess enjoy that most married couples don't is separate bathrooms. Leading off the main bedroom are dressing and bathroom suites for them both. His is large and old-fashioned, with a small single bed in the dressing room on which he takes the occasional nap, while hers is more modern, but is also functional rather than luxurious. One thing they don't have to do is argue about who gets the bathroom first in the morning!

Prince Harry sits on his mother's lap during a photocall at the start of their August 1988 holiday with King Juan Carlos and his family at the Marivent Palace in Palma, Majorca.

From being a baby in his mother's arms on a family cruise on the *Britannia* (right) to holding his grandmother's hand (below right) after the Easter Sunday family service, Prince Harry has always been in the public eye. Even walking to school with big brother Prince William (below) attracted press attention.

The second floor is where the children live. At least, it is where the nursery suite is situated, but in the Wales' household no rooms are held to be sacrosanct. William and Henry are free to roam wherever they like; they do not simply appear once a day, brushed and scrubbed, as royal children in the past would have. In addition to bedrooms and bathrooms for the children and their nannies, there is a tiny kitchen – fish fingers are a favourite – and a day room decorated with postcards sent home by the Prince and Princess from all over the world.

The Princess of Wales grew up in the country, but she spent much of her life in London and openly admits to being a 'city person'. Prince Charles on the other hand says he dislikes London, and most other big cities, and he is at heart a country person, never happier than when he is trudging over his own land, wearing corduroy trousers and Wellington boots. He has often said that he has a house in London but his home is in the country. He is referring to Highgrove House, situated on the outskirts of the pleasant market town of Tetbury, in what has become known as the 'royal' county of Gloucestershire. The Princess Royal and Prince and Princess Michael of Kent also live nearby, forming a triangle of royal homes.

Highgrove is a nine-bedroomed Georgian mansion set in 350 acres of prime agricultural land. The Duchy of Cornwall are technically the owners of the house, having

The Princess of Wales feels a particular empathy with the very young and the very old. Her fondness for children is always in evidence and it is also characteristic of her to imagine herself in other people's shoes and let an elderly lady enjoy the scent of the flowers in her posy.

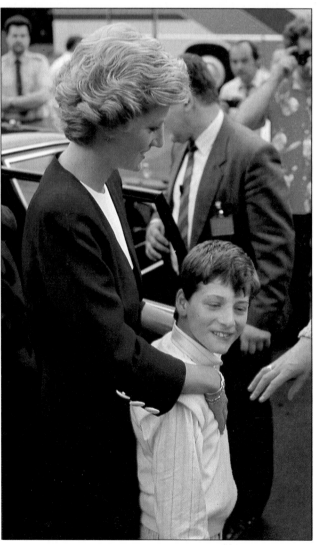

paid around £800,000 for the freehold on behalf of the Prince of Wales. In addition to the nine principal bedrooms, there are six bathrooms, four reception rooms, a swimming pool and one fairly unusual item not normally found in English country houses: a steel-lined room for use in the event of an attack by terrorists. This is on the first floor, and measures twenty feet square; the staff at Highgrove call it the 'iron room' – though it is made entirely of steel. The room has been constructed in such a fashion that, if necessary, the whole room can fall intact onto the ground floor, even if the rest of the house is destroyed. Inside are medical supplies, long-lasting food and drinks, radio transmitters, air purifiers and special lavatories, all of which would enable the occupants to survive inside the 'iron room' for several months.

Prince Charles has said that what finally persuaded him to buy Highgrove was the garden. 'It was a challenge

**Being with children is heaven for Diana – just as it was in her days
at the kindergarten.**

A selection of the Princess's wonderful hats. Diana is famous for her original fashion touches: the turban worn beneath a blue and white hat brim or a tie worn with the blue coat.

to create something,' he said. 'I did rather fall in love with it … the walled garden finally made up my mind.' These days he spends a great deal of his free time in the garden and cheerfully admits that he is becoming a fanatical gardening enthusiast.

Highgrove House was owned by the family of the former prime minister Harold Macmillan (later Earl of Stockton), but it had not been lived in fully for many years before the Prince and Princess of Wales moved in. It was in a very dilapidated state, with a gloomy interior.

This was soon transformed by Dudley Poplak, whose brief was to introduce a light, airy feel while retaining the essentially country house atmosphere favoured by both the Prince and Princess. Soft pastel shades were used in the decoration and colourful chintz fabrics were made up into covers for the chairs and sofas. The overall effect is quite brilliant, making Highgrove a house which is both a suitably elegant royal residence and a welcoming home for a busy couple with two young children.

The Princess's first overseas tour, to Australia in 1983, was a baptism of fire, but the people couldn't have been more welcoming and really took her to their hearts. On that tour, the couple visited the world's largest monolith, Ayers Rock (below). In Canada that same year, the Prince and Princess dressed up in Victorian costumes for a party and singsong at Edmonton celebrating the Gold Rush days.

Many items of furniture and fittings were wedding gifts. The kitchen is all electric and came from one of Germany's leading manufacturers. The china, glassware and cutlery are all wedding presents, each chosen by the Princess, who knew exactly when and where they were going to be used.

Before she was married, the Princess favoured bright colours: vivid pinks, startling yellows and bright blues, so that some of her choices at Highgrove have surprised many of her friends. For instance, all her bedlinen, bath towels and tablecloths are pure white, hardly a practical colour, even for a princess. The entire collection was a gift from the Northern Ireland linen industry, which has a tradition of offering the very best of its products as royal wedding gifts. When someone pointed out to a member

of the staff at Highgrove that white was a difficult colour to keep in pristine condition the reply was immediate, succinct and not without a certain amount of irony: 'That is hardly a consideration in the Princess's case.'

There are four large rooms on the ground floor, including a formal drawing room and a dining room that seats twenty in comfort and in which Prince Charles holds his 'board meetings', when the directors of what is known (behind his back) as 'Prince Charles Limited' gather at Highgrove. Prince Charles' study contains his

An affectionate kiss (above) at the polo ground and playing happy families in Majorca with the families of ex-King Constantine of Greece and their host, King Juan Carlos of Spain.

desk on which is prominently displayed a sign saying 'DO NOT MOVE ANYTHING FROM THIS DESK'. There is also a very comfortable sitting room with a television set and deep armchairs where, at weekends, the Prince and Princess often have their supper served to them.

One of the great difficulties of being royal is that there are few opportunities for being truly alone. Every inch of Highgrove is under constant surveillance by automatic closed-circuit security cameras, even the heated outdoor swimming pool is equipped with a video camera, whose

pictures are monitored from a bank of television screens located in the attic of the main house, which is manned twenty-four hours a day. To make sure their presence is not too obtrusive, the police officers use a special staircase at the rear of the house that leads directly from the attic to the ground floor; this means they can come and go without being seen by the Prince and Princess.

The royal couple are of course fully aware of the need for security and even though they sometimes find it irksome and restricting having to have an armed bodyguard accompany them wherever they go, they accept that this is part of the price they have to pay for

Togetherness in tartan – traditional kilts for Prince Charles, more fashionable interpretations for Princess Diana.

being in the public eye. Prince Charles has become friendly with some of his bodyguards – one of them, Chief Superintendent John Maclean, who was with him for ten years, was closer to the Prince than either of his own brothers. The Princess of Wales, on the other hand, finds their attentions irritating at times, especially when she wants to swim in private. It's impossible to relax when you know that you are being watched constantly by the all-seeing eye of a television camera.

The domestic system at Highgrove has been refined into a smooth-running operation that rarely varies from year to year. The principal staff at Kensington Palace organise their own rotas and allocate weekend duties between themselves. Usually four or five of them, including a butler, valet, chef and the Princess's dresser,

Official duties have their serious and their lighter side. The Princess laughed as she was overwhelmed with garlands during the royal couple's visit to Hong Kong in 1989; they all came from girls related to Gurkha officers stationed at HMS *Tamar* base.

will leave London early on Friday morning in one of the large estate cars, to prepare for the family's arrival later in the day. With the royal engagement books being so full these days, both the Prince and Princess frequently have official duties on Friday, so it is sometimes late evening before they can leave for the weekend. Prince Charles and his wife involve their children in almost everything they do at Highgrove, so before they eat their evening meal together they join William (when he is home from school) and Henry in the nursery for family prayers. This has been the custom since the children were old enough to take part and both parents regard it as an important end to the day and it is something they try never to miss.

The family has breakfast together on Saturday and Sunday mornings, after which Prince Charles can usually be seen around the farm which adjoins Highgrove with one or both of his sons in tow. In the winter, His Royal Highness likes to hunt with one of the local packs, and his children may join in on their ponies; the summer months will often find him pottering in the garden, especially in the vast greenhouses, which are filled with tropical plants and exotic flowers from all over the world. Prince Charles is no armchair gardener either; he enjoys getting his hands dirty and watching something he has planted himself grow to its full size.

Smart day wear and stunning evening gowns are all part of the Princess's public image, and constantly enhance her position as a fashion leader.

Life at Highgrove is not all play, however. The never-ending round of official papers follows him even here, with couriers delivering special boxes of telegrams, letters, documents and reports that have to be dealt with as soon as they arrive. As Prince Charles himself says, 'If I leave them for just one day, the pile just gets bigger.' Nevertheless, Highgrove is where the Prince and Princess and their children are able to behave more as an ordinary family than anywhere else. The extensive grounds offer them a degree of privacy they cannot get in London, or even at Balmoral, where there is always a large household in attendance when the Queen is in residence.

After the stresses and strains of a busy week, whether working together or separately, the royal couple can relax with their family and friends at Highgrove and live as closely as is possible for people in their position to the way in which ordinary married couples live. It would be ridiculous to suggest that they are an ordinary couple, because obviously they are not. But they do share some of the problems the rest of us spend most of our lives trying to cope with. The ailments common to all children did not pass William and Henry by, and the Princess of Wales suffered as much as any other young mother when her children started school. When Prince Charles broke his right arm in several places playing polo, being royal did not stop him from being in as much discomfort as anyone else – nor did it prevent his wife from worrying when he had to spend three hours in the operating theatre after the arm would not heal.

After ten years of marriage both the Prince and Princess of Wales have changed considerably. Of course they have. Who hasn't in ten years? Charles, with his long

The Princess supports and applauds her husband on the polo field, wearing the famous sheep sweater that sported one black sheep knitted into a flock of white ones.

The Queen is very proud of her son and heir, and is clearly delighted to present him with a prize. The Princess may make friends with horses, but is rarely seen on horseback, although she has been riding with the Queen.

habits of introspection and his strongly traditional values, has become the voice of the people in his stand against pollution; pollution of the old values, represented by the falling standards of spoken English and modern architecture and by inner-city decay, as well as the pollution, in real terms, of the very air we breathe, the food we eat and the items we use in our everyday lives. The 'greening' of the Royal Family owes much to Prince Charles. He grows his own vegetables organically and refuses to allow any aerosol containers to be used in any of his homes. In other words, he practises what he preaches. Since marrying his young wife, he has tried to alter his own image – with only slight success. He has not become younger either in appearance or outlook. But he has tried. Through Princess Diana, he has met people he would never have dreamed of meeting socially before: pop stars and actors, alternative comedians and dancers. He is still not completely comfortable in their presence, but nowadays he does not regard them as beings from another planet. The Princess of Wales, meanwhile, has achieved a degree of sophistication in the past ten years that few would have thought possible. Where once she would have giggled in public in order to hide her own nervousness, she now acts in a very calm, down-to-earth

Many of the most relaxed pictures of the royals come, naturally enough, from their more private moments – though for a royal very few moments are entirely private.

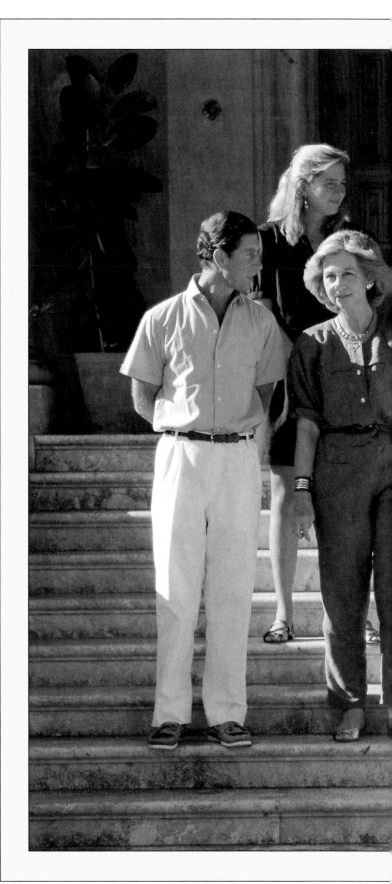

Surrounded by traditionally dressed Arab men and women, the Princess looks to be enjoying herself on a tour of the Middle East.

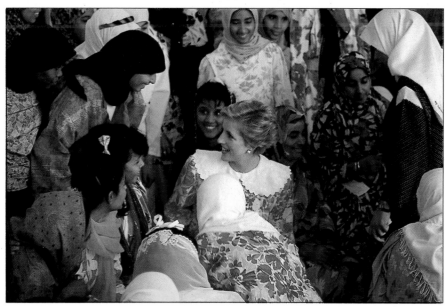

manner. If royal, and married, life has changed her, it has been to make her more mature and more confident: the ideal partner for her husband when he ascends the throne.

As a couple, their relationship has blossomed into a happy, comfortable partnership with each one being aware of, and grateful for, the other's contribution to its success. Charles and Diana are affectionate and loving parents who are determined that their own children will never have to endure the agonies they themselves went through: he, through his chronic shyness and she, because of the break-up of her parents' marriage. They now have the family security they have both always wanted and they will continue to work at keeping it that way.

In their public lives, the Prince and Princess have shown great social concern, involving themselves in the problems of the underprivileged in a way that few others of their generation and class have done and the success of their public partnership has spilled over into their private lives.

So, after several years of doubt and public speculation about whether the Prince and Princess would stay together, all now appears to be calm. They have revealed themselves both as the good-humoured, pragmatic face of royalty and as a loving couple who are coping admirably with the problems of a modern marriage. Whatever happens to them in the future, the next ten years should certainly be easier than the last!

The royal couple travel in a horse-drawn carriage during their historic
trip to the newly-democratic Hungary in 1990. This first official royal visit
to Eastern Europe proved a great success.